A Song Of Hope
copyright © 1993 by Flavia Weedn
All rights reserved. Printed in Hong Kong.

For information write Andrews and McMeel,
a Universal Press Syndicate Company,
4900 Main Street, Kansas City, Missouri 64112

ISBN: 0-8362-4702-7

A Song
Of Hope

Written and Illustrated
by Flavia Weedn

Hope

is

a

gift

we

give

to

ourselves.

FLAVIA

It

is a

free

spirit

whose

silent

song

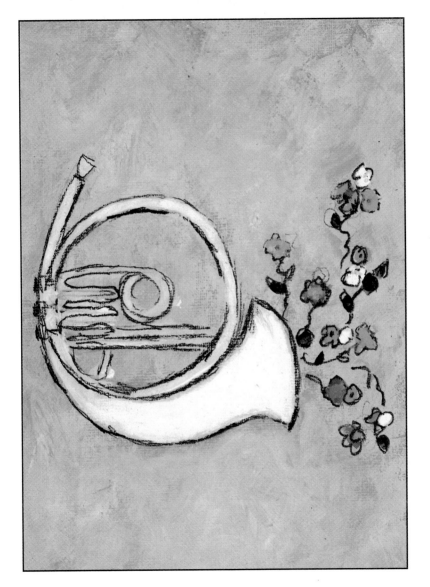

is

of strength

and courage.

It is

a song

of

believing.

of

reaching

for

dreams

and

of never

giving

up.

FLAVIA

Hope is

a gift tied

with ribbons

and

is born

out

of need.

Once you

have it,

it will

never leave you...

FLAVIA

for

it becomes

a part of

what you are.

Although it

may seem

difficult to find...

hope is

always there,

somewhere

in the heart.

Flavia at work in her Santa Barbara studio

Flavia Weedn is a writer, painter and philosopher. Her life's work is about hope for the human spirit. "I want to reach people of all ages who have never been told, 'wait a minute, look around you. It's wonderful to be alive and every one of us matters. We can make a difference if we keep trying and never give up.'" It is Flavia's and her family's wish to awaken this spirit in each and every one of us. Flavia's messages are translated into many foreign languages on giftware, books and paper goods around the world.

To find out more about Flavia write to:
Weedn Studios, Ltd.
740 State Street, 3rd Floor
Santa Barbara, CA 93101 USA
or call: 805-564-6909